The separate works of William H. Davies

Poetry

The Soul's Destroyer. 1906. 4th impression. *Fifield.*
New Poems. 1907. 2nd impression. *Mathews.*
Nature Poems. 1908. 2nd impression; 3rd thousand. *Fifield.*
Farewell to Poesy. 1910. 2nd thousand. *Fifield.*
Songs of Joy. 1911. *Fifield.*
Foliage. 1913. *Mathews.*
The Bird of Paradise. 1914. *Methuen.*
Child Lovers. 1916. 2nd impression. *Fifield.*

Prose

The Autobiography of a Super-Tramp. With Preface by Bernard
   Shaw. 1907. 3rd impression. *Fifield*
A Pilgrim in Wales. 1916. *Melrose.*

Collected Poems

by

William H. Davies

by

William H. Davies

With a portrait in collotype
from a pencil sketch by

WILL ROTHENSTEIN,

and facsimile of author's script

London
A. C. Fifield, 13 Clifford's Inn, E.C.
1916

Note : This single volume
collection of what I believe to
be my best pieces is published in
response to a frequently expressed
wish from the press and public.
For permission to do this, my thanks
are due to the publishers of my
separate volumes of poems —
Mr A. C. Fifield , Mr Elkin Mathews,
and Messrs Methuen & Co.
                              W. H. D.

Contents

Contents

Contents

1.   Thunderstorms

MY mind has thunderstorms,
    That brood for heavy hours
Until they rain me words,
    My thoughts are drooping flowers
And sulking, silent birds.

Yet come, dark thunderstorms,
    And brood your heavy hours;
For when you rain me words,
    My thoughts are dancing flowers
And joyful singing birds.

SING out, my Soul, thy songs of joy;
  Such as a happy bird will sing
Beneath a Rainbow's lovely arch
    In early spring.

Think not of Death in thy young days;
  Why shouldst thou that grim tyrant fear,
And fear him not when thou art old,
    And he is near.

Strive not for gold, for greedy fools
  Measure themselves by poor men never;
Their standard still being richer men,
    Makes them poor ever.

Train up thy mind to feel content,
  What matters then how low thy store?
What we enjoy, and not possess,
    Makes rich or poor.

Filled with sweet thought, then happy I
  Take not my state from others' eyes;
What's in my mind—not on my flesh
    Or theirs, I prize

Sing, happy Soul, thy songs of joy;
    Such as a Brook sings in the wood,
That all night has been strengthened by
    Heaven's purer flood.

3.   The Moon

THY beauty haunts me, heart and soul,
  Oh thou fair Moon, so close and bright;
Thy beauty makes me like the child,
  That cries aloud to own thy light:
The little child that lifts each arm,
To press thee to her bosom warm.

Though there are birds that sing this night
  With thy white beams across their throats,
Let my deep silence speak for me
  More than for them their sweetest notes ·
Who worships thee till music fails
Is greater than thy nightingales.

4.   The Rain

I HEAR leaves drinking Rain;
    I hear rich leaves on top
Giving the poor beneath
    Drop after drop;
'Tis a sweet noise to hear
These green leaves drinking near.

And when the Sun comes out,
    After this Rain shall stop,
A wondrous Light will fill
    Each dark, round drop;
I hope the Sun shines bright:
'Twill be a lovely sight.

5.   Infancy

BORN to the world with my hands clenched,
    I wept and shut my eyes;
Into my mouth a breast was forced,
    To stop my bitter cries.
I did not know—nor cared to know—
    A woman from a man;
Until I saw a sudden light,
    And all my joys began.

From that great hour my hands went forth,
    And I began to prove
That many a thing my two eyes saw
    My hands had power to move :
My fingers now began to work,
    And all my toes likewise;
And reaching out with fingers stretched,
    I laughed, with open eyes.

6. Leisure

WHAT is this life if, full of care,
We have no time to stand and stare.

No time to stand beneath the boughs
And stare as long as sheep or cows.

No time to see, when woods we pass,
Where squirrels hide their nuts in grass.

No time to see, in broad daylight,
Streams full of stars, like stars at night.

No time to turn at Beauty's glance,
And watch her feet, how they can dance.

No time to wait till her mouth can
Enrich that smile her eyes began.

A poor life this if, full of care,
We have no time to stand and stare.

7.   The Visitor

SHE brings that breath, and music too,
    That comes when April's days begin;
And sweetness Autumn never had
    In any bursting skin.

She's big with laughter at the breasts,
    Like netted fish they leap:
O God, that I were far from here,
    Or lying fast asleep!

8.   The Kingfisher

IT was the Rainbow gave thee birth,
   And left thee all her lovely hues;
And, as her mother's name was Tears,
   So runs it in thy blood to choose
For haunts the lonely pools, and keep
In company with trees that weep.

Go you and, with such glorious hues,
   Live with proud Peacocks in green parks;
On lawns as smooth as shining glass,
   Let every feather show its mark;
Get thee on boughs and clap thy wings
Before the windows of proud kings.

Nay, lovely Bird, thou art not vain;
   Thou hast no proud ambitious mind;
I also love a quiet place
   That's green, away from all mankind;
A lonely pool, and let a tree
Sigh with her bosom over me.

9.   The Inexpressible

THINKING of my caged birds indoors,
    My books, whose music serves my will;
Which, when I bid them sing, will sing,
    And when I sing myself are still;

And that my scent is drops of ink,
    Which, were my song as great as I,
Would sweeten man till he was dust,
    And make the world one Araby;

Thinking how my hot passions make
    Strong floods of shallows that run cold—
Oh how I burn to make my dreams
    Lightning and thunder through the world.

SHE walks as lightly as the fly
Skates on the water in July.

To hear her moving petticoat,
For me is music's highest note.

Stones are not heard, when her feet pass,
No more than tumps of moss or grass.

When she sits still, she's like the flower,
To be a butterfly next hour.

The brook laughs not more sweet, when he
Trips over pebbles suddenly.

My Love, like him, can whisper low—
When he comes where green cresses grow.

She rises like the lark, that hour
He goes halfway to meet a shower.

A fresher drink is in her looks
Than Nature gives me, or old books.

When I in my Love's shadow sit,
I do not miss the sun one bit.

When she is near, my arms can hold
All that's worth having in this world.

And when I know not where she is,
Nothing can come but comes amiss.

11. Autumn

AUTUMN grows old; he, like some simple one,
   In Summer's castaway is strangely clad;
Such withered things the winds in frolic mad
Shake from his feeble hand and forehead wan.

Autumn is sighing for his early gold,
   And in his tremble dropping his remains;
   The brook talks more, as one bereft of brains,
Who singeth loud, delirious with the cold.

O now with drowsy June one hour to be !
   Scarce waking strength to hear the hum of bees,
   Or cattle lowing under shady trees,
Knee-deep in waters loitering to the sea.

I would that drowsy June awhile were here,
   The amorous South wind carrying all the vale—
   Save that white lily true to star as pale,
Whose secret day-dream Phœbus burns to hear.

12.   This Night

THIS night, as I sit here alone,
  And brood on what is dead and gone,
The owl that's in this Highgate Wood,
Has found his fellow in my mood;
To every star, as it doth rise—
Oh-o-o! Oh-o-o! he shivering cries.

And, looking at the Moon this night,
There's that dark shadow in her light.
Ah! Life and Death, my fairest one,
Thy lover is a skeleton !
" And why is that ?" I question—"why ? "
Oh-o-o! Oh-o-o! the owl doth cry.

13.   In May

YES, I will spend the livelong day
    With Nature in this month of May;
And sit beneath the trees, and share
My bread with birds whose homes are there;
While cows lie down to eat, and sheep
Stand to their necks in grass so deep;
While birds do sing with all their might,
As though they felt the earth in flight.
This is the hour I dreamed of, when
I sat surrounded by poor men;
And thought of how the Arab sat
Alone at evening, gazing at
The stars that bubbled in clear skies;

And of young dreamers, when their eyes
Enjoyed methought a precious boon
In the adventures of the Moon
Whose light, behind the Clouds' dark bars,
Searched for her stolen flocks of stars.
When I, hemmed in by wrecks of men,
Thought of some lonely cottage then,
Full of sweet books; and miles of sea,
With passing ships, in front of me;
And having, on the other hand,
A flowery, green, bird-singing land

14.   Days too Short

WHEN Primroses are out in Spring,
    And small, blue violets come between;
  When merry birds sing on boughs green,
And rills, as soon as born, must sing;

When butterflies will make side-leaps,
    As though escaped from Nature's hand
    Ere perfect quite; and bees will stand
Upon their heads in fragrant deeps;

When small clouds are so silvery white
    Each seems a broken rimmèd moon—
    When such things are, this world too soon,
For me, doth wear the veil of Night.

15.   The Sleepers

AS I walked down the waterside
   This silent morning, wet and dark;
Before the cocks in farmyards crowed,
   Before the dogs began to bark;
Before the hour of five was struck
By old Westminster's mighty clock:

As I walked down the waterside
   This morning, in the cold damp air,
I saw a hundred women and men
   Huddled in rags and sleeping there:
These people have no work, thought I,
And long before their time they die.

That moment, on the waterside,
   A lighted car came at a bound,
I looked inside, and saw a score
   Of pale and weary men that frowned,
Each man sat in a huddled heap,
Carried to work while fast asleep.

The Sleepers

Ten cars rushed down the waterside,
   Like lighted coffins in the dark;
With twenty dead men in each car,
   That must be brought alive by work :
These people work too hard, thought I,
And long before their time they die.

SIX summers old was she, and when she came
Her head was in an everlasting flame;
The golden fire it licked her neck and face,
But left no mark of soot in any place.

When this young thing had seen her lover boy,
She threw her arms around his neck for joy;
Then, paired like hazel nuts, those two were seen
To make their way towards the meadows green.

Now, to a field they came at last, which was
So full of buttercups they hid the grass;
'Twas fit for kings to meet, and councils hold—
You never saw so fine a cloth of gold.

Then in a while they to a green park came;
A captain owned it, and they knew his name;
And what think you those happy children saw?
The big, black horse that once was in a war.

Now soon she tied her lover with some string,
And laughed, and danced around him in a ring;
He, like a flower that gossamer has tied,

Lord, how she laughed! Her golden ringlets shook
As fast as lambs' tails, when those youngsters suck ;
Sweeter than that enchantress laughed, when she
Shut Merlin fast forever in a tree.

As they went home, that little boy began :
" Love me and, when I'm a big sailor-man,
I'll bring you home more coral, silk, and gold,
Than twenty-five four-funnelled ships could hold.

" And fifty coffins carried to their grave,
Will not have half the lilies you shall have :
Now say at once that you will be my love—
And have a pearl ten stallions could not move."

17. Sweet Stay-at-Home

SWEET Stay-at-Home, sweet Well-content,
   Thou knowest of no strange continent :
Thou hast not felt thy bosom keep
A gentle motion with the deep ;
Thou hast not sailed in Indian seas,
Where scent comes forth in every breeze.
Thou hast not seen the rich grape grow
For miles, as far as eyes can go ;
Thou hast not seen a summer's night
When maids could sew by a worm's light ;
Nor the North Sea in spring send out
Bright hues that like birds flit about
In solid cages of white ice—
Sweet Stay-at-Home, sweet Love-one-place.
Thou hast not seen black fingers pick
White cotton when the bloom is thick,
Nor heard black throats in harmony ;
Nor hast thou sat on stones that lie
Flat on the earth, that once did rise
To hide proud kings from common eyes,
Thou hast not seen plains full of bloom
Where green things had such little room

They pleased the eye like fairer flowers—
Sweet Stay-at-Home, all these long hours.
Sweet Well-content, sweet Love-one-place,
Sweet, simple maid, bless thy dear face;
For thou hast made more homely stuff
Nurture thy gentle self enough;
I love thee for a heart that's kind—
Not for the knowledge in thy mind.

18.   The Elements

NO house of stone
    Was built for me;
When the Sun shines—
    I am a bee.

No sooner comes
    The Rain so warm,
I come to light—
    I am a worm.

When the Winds blow,
    I do not strip,
But set my sails—
    I am a ship

When Lightning comes,
    It plays with me
And I with it—
    I am a tree.

When drowned men rise
    At Thunder's word,
Sings Nightingale—

19.   Come, thou sweet Wonder

COME, thou sweet Wonder, by whose power
　　We more or less enjoy our years;
That mak'st a child forget the breast,
　　And dri'st at once the children's tears,
Till sleep shall bring their minds more rest.

Come to my heavy rain of care,
　　And make it weigh like dew; charm me
With Beauty's hair, her eyes or lips;
　　With mountain dawn, or sunset sea
That's like a thousand burning ships.

HER cruel hands go in and out,
　　Like two pale woodmen working there,
To make a nut-brown thicket clear—
　　The full, wild foliage of her hair.

Her hands now work far up the North,
　　Then, fearing for the South's extreme,
They into her dark waves of hair
　　Dive down so quick—it seems a dream.

They're in the light again with speed,
　　Tossing the loose hair to and fro,
Until, like tamèd snakes, the coils
　　Lie on her bosom in a row.

For wise inspection, up and down
　　One coil her busy hands now run;
To screw and twist, to turn and shape,
　　And here and there to work like one.

And now those white hands, still like one,
　　Are working at the perilous end;
Where they must knot those nut-brown coils,

Sometimes one hand must fetch strange tools,
  The other then must work alone;
But when more instruments are brought,
  They both make up the time that's gone.

Now that her hair is bound secure,
  Coil top of coil, in smaller space,
Ah, now I see how smooth her brow,
  And her simplicity of face.

21.   Day's Black Star

IS it that small black star,
  Twinkling in broad daylight,
Upon the bosom of
  Yon cloud so white—
Is it that small black thing
  Makes earth and all Heaven ring!

Sing, you black star; and soar
  Until, alas! too soon
You fall to earth in one
  Long singing swoon;
But you will rise again
  To Heaven, from this green plain.

Sing, sing, sweet star; though black,
  Your company's more bright
Than any star that shines
  With a white light;
Sing, Skylark, sing; and give
  To me thy joy to live.

22.   The Example

HERE'S an example from
    A Butterfly;
That on a rough, hard rock
    Happy can lie;
Friendless and all alone
    On this unsweetened stone

Now let my bed be hard,
    No care take I;
I'll make my joy like this
    Small Butterfly;
Whose happy heart has power
    To make a stone a flower.

23.   The Likeness

WHEN I came forth this morn I saw
  Quite twenty cloudlets in the air;
And then I saw a flock of sheep,
  Which told me how those clouds came there.

That flock of sheep, on that green grass,
  Well might it lie so still and proud!
Its likeness had been drawn in heaven,
  On a blue sky, in silvery cloud.

I gazed me up, I gazed me down,
  And swore, though good the likeness was,
'Twas a long way from justice done
  To such white wool, such sparkling grass.

24. The Two Children

"AH, little boy! I see
    You have a wooden spade.
Into this sand you dig
    So deep—for what?" I said.
"There's more rich gold," said he,
    "Down under where I stand,
Than twenty elephants
    Could move across the land."

" Ah, little girl with wool!—
    What are you making now?"
"Some stockings for a bird,
    To keep his legs from snow."
And there those children are,
    So happy, small, and proud:
The boy that digs his grave,
    The girl that knits her shroud.

25. The Mind's Liberty

THE mind, with its own eyes and ears,
 May for these others have no care;
No matter where this body is,
 The mind is free to go elsewhere.
My mind can be a sailor, when
 This body's still confined to land;
And turn these mortals into trees,
 That walk in Fleet Street or the Strand.

So, when I'm passing Charing Cross,
 Where porters work both night and day,
I ofttimes hear sweet Malpas Brook,
 That flows thrice fifty miles away.
And when I'm passing near St. Paul's,
 I see, beyond the dome and crowd,
Twm Barlum, that green pap in Gwent,
 With its dark nipple in a cloud.

26.   The Battle

THERE was a battle in her face,
    Between a Lily and a Rose :
My love would have the Lily win
    And I the Lily lose.

I saw with joy that strife, first one,
    And then the other uppermost ;
Until the Rose roused all its blood,
    And then the Lily lost.

When she's alone, the Lily rules,
    By her consent, without mistake :
But when I come that red Rose leaps
    To battle for my sake.

27.   The Lonely Dreamer

HE lives his lonely life, and when he dies
    A thousand hearts maybe will utter sighs;
Because they liked his songs, and now their bird
Sleeps with his head beneath his wing, unheard.

But what kind hand will tend his grave, and bring
Those blossoms there, of which he used to sing?
Who'll kiss his mound, and wish the time would come
To lie with him inside that silent tomb?

And who'll forget the dreamer's skill, and shed
A tear because a loving heart is dead?
Heigh ho for gossip then, and common sighs—
And let his death bring tears to no one's eyes.

28.   The East in Gold

SOMEHOW this world is wonderful at times,
    As it has been from early morn in May;
Since first I heard the cock-a-doodle-do,
    Timekeeper on green farms—at break of day.

Soon after that I heard ten thousand birds,
    Which made me think an angel brought a bin
Of golden grain, and none was scattered yet—
    To rouse those birds to make that merry din.

I could not sleep again, for such wild cries,
    And went out early into their green world;
And then I saw what set their little tongues
    To scream for joy—they saw the East in gold.

29. A Mother to her Sick Child

THOU canst not understand my words,
  No love for me was meant :
The smile that lately crossed thy face
  Was but an accident.

The music's thine, but mine the tears
  That make thy lullaby ;
To-day I'll rock thee into sleep,
  To-morrow thou must die.

And when our babies sleep their last,
  Like agèd dames or men,
They need nor mother's lullaby,
  Nor any rocking then.

30. The Happy Child

I SAW this day sweet flowers grow thick—
But not one like the child did pick.

I heard the packhounds in green park—
But no dog like the child heard bark.

I heard this day bird after bird—
But not one like the child has heard.

A hundred butterflies saw I—
But not one like the child saw fly.

I saw the horses roll in grass—
But no horse like the child saw pass.

My world this day has lovely been—
But not like what the child has seen

31.   To Sparrows Fighting

STOP, feathered bullies !
　　Peace, angry birds ;
You common Sparrows that,
　　For a few words,
Roll fighting in wet mud,
To shed each other's blood.

Look at those Linnets, they
　　Like ladies sing ;
See how those Swallows, too,
　　Play on the wing ;
All other birds close by
Are gentle, clean and shy.

And yet maybe your life's
　　As sweet as theirs ;
The common poor that fight
　　Live not for years
In one long frozen state
　　Of anger, like the great.

32.   The White Cascade

WHAT happy mortal sees that mountain now,
  The white cascade that's shining on its brow;

The white cascade that's both a bird and star,
That has a ten mile voice and shines as far?

Though I may never leave this land again,
Yet every spring my mind must cross the main

To hear and see that water-bird and star
That on the mountain sings, and shines so far.

33.   Nell Barnes

THEY lived apart for three long years,
  Bill Barnes and Nell his wife;
He took his joy from other girls,
  She led a wicked life.

Yet ofttimes she would pass his shop,
  With some strange man awhile;
And, looking, meet her husband's frown
  With her malicious smile.

Until one day, when passing there,
  She saw her man had gone;
And when she saw the empty shop,
  She fell down with a moan.

And when she heard that he had gone
  Five thousand miles away;
And that she'd see his face no more,
  She sickened from that day.

To see his face was health and life,
  And when it was denied,
She could not eat, and broke her heart—
  It was for love she died.

THIS life is sweetest; in this wood
    I hear no children cry for food;
I see no woman white with care,
No man with muscles wasting here.

No doubt it is a selfish thing
To fly from human suffering;
No doubt he is a selfish man,
Who shuns poor creatures sad and wan.

But 'tis a wretched life to face
Hunger in almost every place;
Cursed with a hand that's empty, when
The heart is full to help all men.

Can I admire the statue great,
When living men starve at its feet!
Can I admire the park's green tree,
A roof for homeless misery!

When I can see few men in need,
I then have power to help by deed,

In the Country

For when I am in those great places,
I see ten thousand suffering faces;
Before me stares a wolfish eye,
Behind me creeps a groan or sigh.

SAY what you like,
   All things love me!
I pick no flowers—
   That wins the Bee.

The Summer's Moths
   Think my hand one—
To touch their wings—
   With Wind and Sun.

The garden Mouse
   Comes near to play;
Indeed, he turns
   His eyes away.

The Wren knows well
   I rob no nest;
When I look in,
   She still will rest.

The hedge stops Cows.
   Or they would come
After my voice

The Horse can tell,
  Straight from my lip,
My hand could not
  Hold any whip.

Say what you like,
  All things love me!
Horse, Cow, and Mouse,
  Bird, Moth, and Bee.

36.   The Flood

I THOUGHT my true love slept;
  Behind her chair I crept
    And pulled out a long pin;
The golden flood came out,
She shook it all about,
    With both our faces in.

Ah! little wren, I know
Your mossy, small nest now
    A windy, cold place is;
No eye can see my face,
Howe'er it watch the place
    Where I half drown in bliss.

When I am drowned half dead,
She laughs and shakes her head;
    Flogged by her hair-waves, I
Withdraw my face from there;
But never once, I swear,
    She heard a mercy-cry.

37. Christ the Man

LORD, I say nothing; I profess
  No faith in Thee nor Christ Thy Son :
Yet no man ever heard me mock
  A true believing one.

If knowledge is not great enough
  To give a man believing power,
Lord, he must wait in Thy great hand
  Till revelation's hour.

Meanwhile he'll follow Christ the man,
  In that humanity he taught,
Which to the poor and the oppressed,
  Gives its best time and thought.

I KNOW not why I yearn for thee again,
  To sail once more upon thy fickle flood;
I'll hear thy waves wash under my death-bed,
  Thy salt is lodged forever in my blood.

Yet I have seen thee lash the vessel's sides
  In fury, with thy many tailèd whip;
And I have seen thee, too, like Galilee,
  When Jesus walked in peace to Simon's ship.

And I have seen thy gentle breeze as soft
  As summer's, when it makes the cornfields run;
And I have seen thy rude and lusty gale
  Make ships show half their bellies to the sun.

Thou knowest the way to tame the wildest life,
  Thou knowest the way to bend the great and proud:
I think of that Armada whose puffed sails,
  Greedy and large, came swallowing every cloud.

But I have seen the sea-boy, young and drowned,
  Lying on shore and, by thy cruel hand,
A seaweed beard was on his tender chin,

And yet, for all, I yearn for thee again,
  To sail once more upon thy fickle flood :
I'll hear thy waves wash under my death-bed,
  Thy salt is lodged forever in my blood.

39.   A Great Time

SWEET Chance, that led my steps abroad,
    Beyond the town, where wild flowers grow—
A rainbow and a cuckoo, Lord,
   How rich and great the times are now !
     Know, all ye sheep
     And cows, that keep
On staring that I stand so long
   In grass that's wet from heavy rain—
A rainbow and a cuckoo's song
   May never come together again ;
     May never come
     This side the tomb.

40.   Man

I SAW Time running by—
  Stop, Thief, was all the cry.
I heard a voice say, Peace!
Let this vain clamour cease.
Can ye bring lightning back
That leaves upon its track
Men, horses, oak trees dead?
Canst bring back Time? it said.
There's nothing in Man's mind
Can catch Time up behind;
In front of that fast Thief
There's no one—end this grief.
Tut, what is Man? How frail!
A grain, a little nail,
The wind, a change of cloth—
A fly can give him death.
Some fishes in the sea
Are born to outlive thee,
And owls, and toads, and trees—
And is Man more than these?
I see Man's face in all

I see the face of him
In things that fly or swim;
One fate for all, I see—
Whatever that may be.
Imagination fits
Life to a day; though its
Length were a thousand years,
'Twould not decrease our fears:
What strikes men cold and dumb
Is that Death's time *must* come.

41.   Truly Great

MY walls outside must have some flowers,
   My walls within must have some books;
A house that's small; a garden large,
   And in it leafy nooks.

A little gold that's sure each week;
   That comes not from my living kind,
But from a dead man in his grave,
   Who cannot change his mind.

A lovely wife, and gentle too;
   Contented that no eyes but mine
Can see her many charms, nor voice
   To call her beauty fine.

Where she would in that stone cage live,
   A self-made prisoner, with me;
While many a wild bird sang around,
   On gate, on bush, on tree.

And she sometimes to answer them,
   In her far sweeter voice than all;
Till birds, that loved to look on leaves,

Truly Great

With this small house, this garden large,
  This little gold, this lovely mate,
With health in body, peace at heart—
  Show me a man more great.

42.   The Sluggard

A JAR of cider and my pipe,
   In summer, under shady tree;
A book of one that made his mind
   Live by its sweet simplicity :
Then must I laugh at kings who sit
   In richest chambers, signing scrolls ;
And princes cheered in public ways,
   And stared at by a thousand fools.

Let me be free to wear my dreams,
   Like weeds in some mad maiden's hair,
When she believes the earth has not
   Another maid so rich and fair ;
And proudly smiles on rich and poor,
   The queen of all fair women then :
So I, dressed in my idle dreams,
   Will think myself the king of men.

43.   When on a Summer's Morn

WHEN on a summer's morn I wake,
  And open my two eyes,
Out to the clear, born-singing rills
  My bird-like spirit flies ;

To hear the Blackbird, Cuckoo, Thrush,
  Or any bird in song ;
And common leaves that hum all day,
  Without a throat or tongue.

And when Time strikes the hour for sleep,
  Back in my room alone,
My heart has many a sweet bird's song—
  And one that's all my own.

44.   Farewell to Poesy

SWEET Poesy, why art thou dumb!
   I loved thee as my captive bird,
That sang me songs when spring was gone,
   And birds of freedom were not heard;
Nor dreamt thou wouldst turn false and cold
   When needed most, by men grown old.

Sweet Poesy, why art thou dumb!
   I fear thy singing days are done;
The poet in my soul is dying,
   And every charm in life is gone;
In vain birds scold and flowers do plead- -
   The poet dies, his heart doth bleed.

45. Early Morn

WHEN I did wake this morn from sleep,
It seemed I heard birds in a dream;
Then I arose to take the air—
The lovely air that made birds scream;
Just as a green hill launched the ship
Of gold, to take its first clear dip.

And it began its journey then,
As I came forth to take the air;
The timid Stars had vanished quite,
The Moon was dying with a stare;
Horses, and kine, and sheep were seen
As still as pictures, in fields green.

It seemed as though I had surprised
And trespassed in a golden world
That should have passed while men still slept!
The joyful birds, the ship of gold,
The horses, kine and sheep did seem
As they would vanish for a dream.

46. Robin Redbreast

ROBIN on a leafless bough,
Lord in Heaven, how he sings!
Now cold Winter's cruel Wind
Makes playmates of withered things.

How he sings for joy this morn!
How his breast doth pant and glow!
Look you how he stands and sings,
Half-way up his legs in snow!

If these crumbs of bread were pearls,
And I had no bread at home,
He should have them for that song;
Pretty Robin Redbreast, Come.

47. A Lovely Woman

NOW I can see what Helen was :
   Men cannot see this woman pass
And be not stirred; as Summer's Breeze
Sets leaves in battle on the trees.
A woman moving gracefully,
With golden hair enough for three,
Which, mercifully! is not loose,
But lies in coils to her head close;
With lovely eyes, so dark and blue,
So deep, so warm, they burn me through.
I see men follow her, as though
Their homes were where her steps should go.
She seemed as sent to our cold race
For fear the beauty of her face
Made Paradise in flames like Troy—
I could have gazed all day with joy.
In fancy I could see her stand
Before a savage, fighting band,
And make them, with her words and looks,
Exchange their spears for shepherd's crooks,
And sing to sheep in quiet nooks;

A Lovely Woman

In fancy saw her beauty make
A thousand gentle priests uptake
Arms for her sake, and shed men's blood.
The fairest piece of womanhood,
Lovely in feature, form and grace,
I ever saw, in any place.

THEY'RE creeping on the stairs outside,
   They're whispering soft and low;
Now up, now down, I hear his friends,
   And still they come and go.

The sweat that runs my side, from that
   Hot pit beneath my shoulder,
Is not so cold as he will be,
   Before the night's much older.

My fire I feed with naked hands,
   No sound shall reach their ears;
I'm moving like the careful cat,
   That stalks a rat it fears.

And as his friends still come and go,
   A thoughtful head is mine :
Had Life as many friends as Death,
   Lord, how this world would shine !

And since I'll have so many friends,
   When on my death-bed lying--
I wish my life had more love now,

49.   The Laughers

MARY and Maud have met at the door,
   Oh, now for a din; I told you so:
They're laughing at once with sweet, round mouths,
   Laughing for what? does anyone know?

Is it known to the bird in the cage,
   That he shrieks for joy his high top notes,
After a silence so long and grave—
   What started at once those two sweet throats?

Is it known to the Wind that he takes
   Advantage at once and comes right in?
Is it known to the cock in the yard,
   That crows—the cause of that merry din?

Is it known to the babe that he shouts?
   Is it known to the old, purring cat?
Is it known to the dog, that he barks
   For joy—what Mary and Maud laugh at?

Is it known to themselves?   It is not,
   But beware of their great shining eyes;
For Mary and Maud will soon, I swear,
   Find a cause to make far merrier cries.

50.   The Boy

GO, little boy,
    Fill thee with joy;
    For Time gives thee
Unlicensed hours,
    To run in fields,
And roll in flowers.

A little boy
Can life enjoy;
    If but to see
The horses pass,
    When shut indoors
Behind the glass.

Go, little boy,
Fill thee with joy;
    Fear not, like man,
The kick of wrath,
    That you do lie
In some one's path.

Time is to thee
Eternity,
   As to a bird
Or butterfly;
   And in that faith
True joy doth lie.

AND now, when merry winds do blow,
   And rain makes trees look fresh,
An overpowering staleness holds
   This mortal flesh.

Though well I love to feel the rain,
   And be by winds well blown—
The mystery of mortal life
   Doth press me down.

And, in this mood, come now what will,
   Shine Rainbow, Cuckoo call;
There is no thing in Heaven or Earth
   Can lift my soul.

I know not where this state comes from—
   No cause for grief I know;
The Earth around is fresh and green,
   Flowers near me grow.

I sit between two fair Rose trees;
   Red roses on my right,
And on my left side roses are

The Dark Hour

The little birds are full of joy,
  Lambs bleating all the day;
The colt runs after the old mare,
  And children play.

And still there comes this dark, dark hour—
  Which is not born of Care;
Into my heart it creeps before
  I am aware.

52.   Jenny Wren

HER sight is short, she comes quite near;
   A foot to me's a mile to her ;
And she is known as Jenny Wren,
The smallest bird in England.   When
I heard that little bird at first,
Methought her frame would surely burst
With earnest song.   Oft had I seen
Her running under leaves so green,
Or in the grass when fresh and wet,
As though her wings she would forget.
And, seeing this, I said to her—
" My pretty runner, you prefer
To be a thing to run unheard
Through leaves and grass, and not a bird ! "
'Twas then she burst, to prove me wrong,
Into a sudden storm of song ;
So very loud and earnest, I
Feared she would break her heart and die.
" Nay, nay," I laughed, " be you no thing
To run unheard, sweet scold, but sing !
O I could hear your voice near me,
Above the din in that oak tree,
When almost all the twigs on top
Had starlings chattering without stop."

53.   Kitty and I

THE gentle wind that waves
    The green boughs here and there
Is showing how my hand
    Waved Kitty's finer hair

The Bee, when all his joints
    Are clinging to a Blossom,
Is showing how I clung
    To Kitty's softer bosom.

The Rill, when his sweet voice
    Is hushed by water-cresses,
Is Kitty's sweeter voice
    Subdued by my long kisses.

Those little stars that shine
    So happy in the skies,
Are those sweet babes I saw
    Whose heaven was Kitty's eyes.

The Moon, that casts her beam
    Upon the hill's dark crest,
Is Kitty's whiter arm
    Across my hairy breast.

Kitty and I

The hazel nuts, when paired
   Unseen beneath the boughs,
Are Kitty and myself,
   Whenever Chance allows.

54.   A Drinking Song

A BEE goes mumbling homeward pleased,
He has not slaved away his hours;
He's drunken with a thousand healths
Of love and kind regard for flowers.
Pour out the wine,
His joy be mine.

Forgetful of affairs at home,
He has sipped oft and merrily;
Forgetful of his duty—Oh!
What can he say to his queen bee?
He says in wine,
" Boo to her shrine ! "

The coward dog that wags his tail,
And rubs the nose with mangy curs,
And fearful says, " Come play, not fight,"
Knows not the draught to drown his fears;
Knows not the wine,
The ruby shine.

A Drinking Song

Poor beggar, breathless in yon barn,
Who fears a mouse to move thy straw,
Must Conscience pester thee all night,
And fear oppress with thoughts of law?
O dearth of wine,
No sleep is thine.

Is Bacchus not the god of gods,
Who gives to Beauty's cheeks their shine?
O Love, thou art a wingless worm;
Wouldst thou be winged, fill thee with wine;
Fill thee with wine,
And wings be thine.

Then, Bacchus, rule thy merry race,
And laws like thine who would not keep?
And when fools weep to hear us laugh,
We'll laugh, ha! ha! to see them weep.
O god of wine,
My soul be thine.

55. Money

WHEN I had money, money, O!
    I knew no joy till I went poor;
For many a false man as a friend
    Came knocking all day at my door.

Then felt I like a child that holds
    A trumpet that he must not blow
Because a man is dead; I dared
    Not speak to let this false world know.

Much have I thought of life, and seen
    How poor men's hearts are ever light;
And how their wives do hum like bees
    About their work from morn till night.

So, when I hear these poor ones laugh,
    And see the rich ones coldly frown—
Poor men, think I, need not go up
    So much as rich men should come down.

When I had money, money, O!
    My many friends proved all untrue;
But now I have no money, O!
    My friends are real, though very few.

56.   Sadness and Joy

I PRAY you, Sadness, leave me soon,
  In sweet invention thou art poor !
Thy sister, Joy, can make ten songs
  While thou art making four.

One hour with thee is sweet enough ;
  But when we find the whole day gone
And no created thing is left—
  We mourn the evil done.

Thou art too slow to shape thy thoughts
  In stone, on canvas, or in song ;
But Joy, being full of active heat,
  Must do some deed ere long.

Thy sighs are gentle, sweet thy tears ;
  But if thou canst not help a man
To prove in substance what he feels—
  Then give me Joy, who can.

Therefore, sweet Sadness, leave me soon,
  Let thy bright sister, Joy, come more ;
For she can make ten lovely songs
  While thou art making four.

57. Fancy's Home

TELL me, Fancy, sweetest child,
    Of thy parents and thy birth;
Had they silk, and had they gold,
    And a park to wander forth,
With a castle green and old?

In a cottage I was born,
    My kind father was Content,
My dear mother Innocence;
    On wild fruits of wonderment
I have nourished ever since.

58. Happy Wind

OH, happy wind, how sweet
    Thy life must be!
The great, proud fields of gold
    Run after thee:
And here are flowers, with heads
    To nod and shake;
And dreaming butterflies
    To tease and wake.
Oh, happy wind, I say,
To be alive this day.

59. Sleep

LIFE'S angel half, sweet Sleep,
  When, like the mermaid, thou
In all thy loveliness
Dost rise from out the deep
Where Life is foul to see—
Men wake to scheme and sin,
But thou dost keep them pure
In that sweet hour with thee.

The flower upon the hill,
Where caves and crags and peaks
Carry the thunder on
After the heavens are still,
Knows thee : as that cared flower
Within some sheltering wood,
And houses built by men,
And in a lady's bower.

If Age hath followed Truth,
A conscience clean and pure

But Age and Innocence
Dost thou, sweet Sleep, reward :
Thou givest rest to both,
To both art recompense.

Yet thou hast awful power
When thou art lying still
And breathing quietly !
Was it not such an hour
Dark Murder slunk away,
Fearing thy innocence
More than the watchfulness
Of men in armed array ?

Thou makest War to cease
Awhile, and armies pause ;
And in the midst of strife
Thou bringest them to peace ;
The tyrant must delay
The cruel deed at thy command ;
Oppressed ones know thy balm
Can take their fears away.

60.   When I am Old

WHEN I am old, and it is spring,
　　And joy leaps dancing, wild and free,
Clear out of every living thing,
　　While I command no ecstasy;
And to translate the songs of birds
Will be beyond my power in words:

When time serves notice on my Muse
　　To leave at last her lyric home,
With no extension of her lease—
　　Then to the blackest pits I come,
To see by day the star's cold light,
And in my coffin sleep at night.

For when these little songs shall fail,
　　These happy notes that to the world
Are puny mole-hills, nothing more,
　　That unto me are Alps of gold—
That toad's dark life must be my own,
Buried alive inside a stone.

61.   Joy and Pleasure

NOW, Joy is born of parents poor,
    And Pleasure of our richer kind;
Though Pleasure's free, she cannot sing
    As sweet a song as Joy confined.

Pleasure's a Moth, that sleeps by day
    And dances by false glare at night;
But Joy's a Butterfly, that loves
    To spread its wings in Nature's light.

Joy's like a Bee that gently sucks
    Away on blossoms its sweet hour;
But Pleasure's like a greedy Wasp,
    That plums and cherries would devour.

Joy's like a Lark that lives alone,
    Whose ties are very strong, though few;
But Pleasure like a Cuckoo roams,
    Makes much acquaintance, no friends true.

Joy from her heart doth sing at home,
    With little care if others hear;
But Pleasure then is cold and dumb,
    And sings and laughs with strangers near.

62.   The Heap of Rags

ONE night when I went down
    Thames' side, in London Town,
A heap of rags saw I,
And sat me down close by.
That thing could shout and bawl,
But showed no face at all;
When any steamer passed
And blew a loud shrill blast,
That heap of rags would sit
And make a sound like it;
When struck the clock's deep bell,
It made those peals as well.
When winds did moan around,
It mocked them with that sound;
When all was quiet, it
Fell into a strange fit;
Would sigh, and moan and roar,
It laughed, and blessed, and swore.
Yet that poor thing, I know,
Had neither friend nor foe;
Its blessing or its curse
Made no one better or worse.

The Heap of Rags

I left it in that place—
The thing that showed no face
Was it a man that had
Suffered till he went mad?
So many showers and not
One rainbow in the lot;
Too many bitter fears
To make a pearl from tears.

63.   The Hawk

THOU dost not fly, thou art not perched,
   The air is all around :
What is it that can keep thee set,
   From falling to the ground ?
The concentration of thy mind
   Supports thee in the air ;
As thou dost watch the small young birds,
   With such a deadly care.

My mind has such a hawk as thou,
   It is an evil mood ;
It comes when there's no cause for grief,
   And on my joys doth brood.
Then do I see my life in parts ;
   The earth receives my bones,
The common air absorbs my mind—
   It knows not flowers from stones.

64.   The Weeping Child

WHAT makes thee weep so, little child,
  What cause hast thou for all this grief ?
When thou art old much cause may be,
  And tears will bring thee no relief.

Thou dost not know thy mother yet,
  Thou'dst sleep on any bosom near ;
Thou dost not see a daughter dying,
  No son is coughing in thy ear.

Thy father is a bearded man,
  Yet any bearded man could take
Thee in his arms, and thou not know
  Which man would die for thy sweet sake.

What makes thee weep then, little child,
  What cause hast thou for all this bother ;
Whose father could be any man,
  And any woman be thy mother ?

65. Seeking Beauty

COLD winds can never freeze, nor thunder sour
   The cup of cheer that Beauty draws for me
Out of those azure Heavens and this green earth—
   I drink and drink, and thirst the more I see.

To see the dewdrops thrill the blades of grass,
   Makes my whole body shake; for here's my choice
Of either sun or shade, and both are green—
   A Chaffinch laughs in his melodious voice.

The banks are stormed by Speedwell, that blue flower
   So like a little Heaven with one star out;
I see an amber lake of Buttercups,
   And Hawthorn foams the hedges round about.

The old Oak tree looks now so green and young,
   That even swallows perch awhile and sing:
This is that time of year, so sweet and warm,
   When Bats wait not for Stars ere they take wing.

As long as I love Beauty I am young,
   Am young or old as I love more or less;
When Beauty is not heeded or seems stale,
   My life's a cheat, let Death end my distress.

66.   The Hermit

WHAT moves that lonely man is not the boom
    Of waves that break against the cliff so strong;
Nor roar of thunder, when that travelling voice
    Is caught by rocks that carry far along.

'Tis not the groan of oak tree in its prime,
    When lightning strikes its solid heart to dust;
Nor frozen pond when, melted by the sun,
    It suddenly doth break its sparkling crust.

What moves that man is when the blind bat taps
    His window when he sits alone at night;
Or when the small bird sounds like some great beast
    Among the dead, dry leaves so frail and light.

Or when the moths on his night-pillow beat
    Such heavy blows he fears they'll break his bones;
Or when a mouse inside the papered walls,
    Comes like a tiger crunching through the stones.

WHEN I was once in Baltimore
    A man came up to me and cried,
"Come, I have eighteen hundred sheep,
    And we will sail on Tuesday's tide.

"If you will sail with me, young man,
    I'll pay you fifty shillings down;
These eighteen hundred sheep I take
    From Baltimore to Glasgow town."

He paid me fifty shillings down,
    I sailed with eighteen hundred sheep;
We soon had cleared the harbour's mouth,
    We soon were in the salt sea deep.

The first night we were out at sea
    Those sheep were quiet in their mind;
The second night they cried with fear—
    They smelt no pastures in the wind.

They sniffed, poor things, for their green fields,
    They cried so loud I could not sleep:
For fifty thousand shillings down

68. The Idiot and the Child

THERE was a house where an old dame
   Lived with a son, his child and wife;
And with a son of fifty years,
   An idiot all his life.

When others wept this idiot laughed,
   When others laughed he then would weep;
The married pair took oath his eyes
   Did never close in sleep.

Death came that way, and which think you
   Fell under that old tyrant's spell?
He breathed upon that little child,
   Who loved her life so well.

This made the idiot chuckle hard:
   The old dame looked at that child dead
And him she loved—"Ah, well; thank God
   It is no worse!" she said.

69. Starers

THE small birds peck at apples ripe,
  And twice as big as them in size;
The wind doth make the hedge's leaves
  Shiver with joy, until it dies.
Young Gossamer is in the field;
  He holds the flowers with silver line—
They nod their heads as horses should.
  And there are forty dappled kine
As fat as snails in deep, dark wells,
  And just as shiny too—as they
Lie in a green field, motionless,
  And every one now stares my way.
I must become a starer too:
  I stare at them as urchins can
When seamen talk, or any child
  That sees by chance its first black man.
I stare at drops of rain that shine
  Like glowworms, when the time is noon;
I stare at little stars in Heaven,
  That try to stare like the big Moon.

70.   Plants and Men

YOU berries once,
In early hours,
Were pretty buds,
And then fair flowers.

Drop, drop at once,
Your life is done;
You cannot feel
The dew or sun.

We are the same,
First buds, then flowers;
Hard berries then,
In our last hours.

Sweet buds, fair flowers,
Hard berries then—
Such is the life
Of plants and men.

71.   The One Singer

DEAD leaves from off the tree
    Make whirlpools on the ground,
Like dogs that chase their tails,
    Those leaves go round and round;
Like birds unfledged and young,
    The old bare branches cry;
Branches that shake and bend
    To feel the winds go by.

No other sound is heard,
    Save from those boughs so bare—
Hark ! who sings that one song ?
    'Tis Robin sings so rare.
How sweet ! like those sad tunes
    In homes where grief's not known;
Or that a blind girl sings
    When she is left alone.

72.   Lines from
" The Soul's Destroyer "

WE went together side by side to school,
    Together had our holidays in fields
Made golden by June's buttercups ; in woods,
Where under ferns fresh pulled I buried her,
And called her forth like Lazarus from the grave ;
She'd laughing come, to shake her curls until
Methought to hear full half a hundred bells
A grown-up world took playful notice soon,
Made me feel shame that grew a greater love ;
She was more chary of her laughter then,
And more subdued her voice, as soft and sweet
As Autumn's, blowing through his golden reeds.
In her sweet sympathies she was a woman
When scarcely she was more than child in years ;
And yet one angry moment parted us,
And days of longing never joined us more.

73.   April's Charms

WHEN April scatters coins of primrose gold
    Among the copper leaves in thickets old,
And singing skylarks from the meadows rise,
To twinkle like black stars in sunny skies;

When I can hear the small woodpecker ring
Time on a tree for all the birds that sing;
And hear the pleasant cuckoo, loud and long—
The simple bird that thinks two notes a song;

When I can hear the woodland brook, that could
Not drown a babe, with all his threatening mood;
Upon whose banks the violets make their home,
And let a few small strawberry blossoms come:

When I go forth on such a pleasant day,
One breath outdoors takes all my care away;
It goes like heavy smoke, when flames take hold
Of wood that's green, and fills a grate with gold.

74. The Call of the Sea

GONE are the days of canvas sails !
No more great sailors tell their tales
In country taverns, barter pearls
For kisses from strange little girls ;
And when the landlord's merry daughter
Heard their rough jokes and shrieked with laughter,
They threw a muffler of rare fur,
That hid her neck from ear to ear.
Ho, ho ! my merry men ; they know
Where gold is plentiful—Sail ho !
How they did love the rude wild Sea !
The rude, unflattering Sea ; for he
Will not lie down for monarch's yacht,
No more than merchant's barge ; he'll not
Keep graves with marks of wood or stone
For fish or fowl, or human bone.
The Sea is loth to lose a friend ;
Men of one voyage, when they spend
Six months with him, hear his vexed cry
Haunting their houses till they die.
And for the sake of him they let
The winds blow them, and raindrops wet

Their foreheads with fresh water sprays—
Thinking of his wild, salty days.
And well they love to saunter near
A river, and its motion hear;
And see ships lying in calm beds,
That danced upon seas' living heads;
And in their dreams they hear again
Men's voices in a hurricane—
Like ghosts complaining that their graves
Are moved by sacrilegious waves.
And well they love to stand and hear
The old seafaring men that fear
Land more than water; carts and trains
More than wild waves and hurricanes.
And they will walk with love and pride
The tattooed mariner beside—
Chains, anchors on his arm, and ships—
And listen to his bearded lips.
Aye, they will hear the Sea's vexed cry
Haunting their houses till they die.

75. Her Absence

HOW rich hath Time become through her.
　　His sands are turned to purest gold!
And yet it grieves my heart full sore
　　To see them slipping from my hold.
How precious now each moment is,
　　Which I must cast like ash away!
My only hope and comfort this—
　　Each moment will return that day,
On that blest day, that joyful hour
When she lies willing in my power.

Nay, these rich moments are not lost,
　　But, like the morning's dewdrops, which
Into the sun their brief lives cast,
　　To make his body far more rich—
So do these precious moments glide
　　Into her being, where they store;
Until I clasp her as my bride,
　　And get them back with thousands more,
Where they have banked in her dear breast,
And saved themselves with interest.

76.   The Dreaming Boy

SWEET are thy dreams, thou happy, careless boy;
Thou know'st the taste of immortality;
No weary limbs can rest upon thy heart;
Sleep has no care to ease thee of at night;
The same move shuts together eye and mind,
And in the morning one move opens both.
Life lies before thee, hardly stepped on yet,
Like a green prairie, fresh, and full of flowers.
Life lies before thee for experiment,
Until old age comes, whose sad eyes can trace
A better path he missed, with fairer flowers,
Which other men have walked in misery.
Thou hast no knowledge of a life of toil,
How hard Necessity destroys our dreams,
And castles in the air must pay him tithes
So heavy that no tenant keeps them long.
To thee the world is still unknown and strange;
Still full of wild romance, as in those days
Ere England launched her forests on the sea.
Thou wilt discover in far mountain caves
Deserted, lamps left burning for thy feet,
And comfort in them more than kings are worth.
Aye, many a gate will open at thy call.

And wise men will come forth to welcome thee,
And bells will ring for pleasure in thy ear
Great monsters in dark woods, with mighty mouths
That swallow their own faces when they yawn,
And mountain bears that carry on their backs
Rough, shaggy coats whose price compares with silk—
Will fall by thy strong, right, all-conquering arm.
And who can stop thee; who can turn thee back?
Not giants, though they stand full twenty feet,
And sit too tall for common men to stand.
Oh, that sweet magic in thee, happy boy!
It makes a golden world for all things young.
Thou with an iron ring, a piece of bone,
A rusty blade, or half a yard of rope,
Art richer than a man with mines and ships.
The child's fresh mind makes honey out of soot,
Sweeter than Age can make on banks of flowers;
He needs but cross a bridge, that happy boy,
And he can breathe the air of a new world.
Sweet children, with your trust in this hard life—
Like little birds that ope their mouths for food
From hands that come to cage them till they die.

77.   The Power of Music

O THOSE sweet notes, so soft and faint; that seemed
  Locked up inside a thick-walled house of stone;
And then that sudden rush of sound, as though
  The doors and windows were wide-open thrown.

Do with me, O sweet music, as thou wilt,
  I am thy slave to either laugh or weep;
Thy power can make thy slave a lover proud,
  Or friendless man that has no place to sleep.

I hear thy gentle whisper and again
  Hear ripples lap the quays of sheltered docks;
I hear thy thunder and it brings to mind
  Dark Colorado scaling his huge rocks.

I hear thy joyous cries and think of birds
  Delirious when the sun doth rise in May;
I hear thy moans and think me of poor cows
  That miss at night the calves they licked by day.

I hear thee wail and think of that sad queen
  Who saw her lover's disappearing mast;
How she, who drank and wasted a rich pearl—
  To prove her love—was left to wail at last.

Do with me, O sweet Music, as thou wilt;
Till even thou art robbed by jealous Sleep
Of those sweet senses thou hast forced from me-
And I can neither laugh with thee nor weep.

78. The Muse

I HAVE no ale,
  No wine I want;
No ornaments,
  My meat is scant.

No maid is near,
  I have no wife;
But here's my pipe
  And, on my life:

With it to smoke,
  And woo the Muse,
To be a king
  I would not choose.

But I crave all,
  When she does fail—
Wife, ornaments,
  Meat, wine and ale.

79. The Owl

THE boding Owl, that in despair
  Doth moan and shiver on warm nights—
Shall that bird prophesy for me
  The fall of Heaven's eternal lights?

When in the thistled field of Age
  I take my final walk on earth
Still will I make that Owl's despair
  A thing to fill my heart with mirth.

80.   My Lady Comes

PEACE, mournful Bee, with that
　　Man's deep voice from the grave:
My Lady comes, and Flowers
　　Make all their colours wave;
And joyful shivers seize
The hedges, grass and trees.

My Lady comes, and Leaves
　　Above her head clap hands;
The Cow stares o'er the field,
　　Up straight the Horse now stands;
Under her loving eyes
Flowers change to Butterflies.

The Grass comes running up
　　To kiss her coming feet;
Then cease your grumble, Bee,
　　When I my Lady meet;
And Arch, let not your stones
Turn our soft sighs to groans.

81.   The Daisy

I KNOW not why thy beauty should
 Remind me of the cold, dark grave—
Thou Flower, as fair as Moonlight, when
 She kissed the mouth of a black Cave.

All other Flowers can coax the Bees,
 All other Flowers are sought but thee:
Dost thou remind them all of Death,
 Sweet Flower, as thou remindest Me?

Thou seemest like a blessèd ghost,
 So white, so cold, though crowned with gold;
Among these glazèd Buttercups,
 And purple Thistles, rough and bold.

When I am dead, nor thought of more,
 And gone from human memory—
Grow you on my forsaken grave,
 And win for me a stranger's sigh.

A day or two the lilies fade;
 A month, aye less, no friends are seen.
Then, claimant to forgotten graves,
 Share my lost place with the wild green.

82.   Fairies, take Care

A THOUSAND blessings, Puck, on you
For knotting that long grass which threw
Into my arms a maid; for we
Have told our love and kissed, and she
Will lie a-bed in a sweet fright.
So, all ye Fairies who to-night
May take that stormy passage where
Her bosom's quicksands are, take care
Of whirlpools too: beware all you
Of that great tempest Love must brew.
The waves will rock your breath near out;
First sunk, then tossed and rolled about,
Now on your heads, now on your feet—.
You'll be near swamped and, for life sweet,
Be glad to cross that stormy main,
And stand on something firm again.
Would I could see her while she sleeps,
And smiles to feel you climb those steeps,
Where you at last will stand up clear
Upon their cherry tops, and cheer.
And that ye are not lost, take care,
In that deep forest of her hair:
Yet ye may enter naked stark,
It gets more warm as it gets dark.
So, Fairies, fear not any harm,
While in those woods so dark and warm.

HER baby brother laughed last night,
   The blind child asked her mother why;
It was the light that caught his eye.
   Would she might laugh to see that light!

The presence of a stiffened corse
   Is sad enough; but, to my mind,
   The presence of a child that's blind,
In a green garden, is far worse.

She felt my cloth—for worldly place;
   She felt my face—if I was good;
   My face lost more than half its blood,
For fear her hand would wrongly trace.

We're in the garden, where are bees
   And flowers, and birds, and butterflies;
   One greedy fledgling runs and cries
For all the food his parent sees!

I see them all: flowers of all kind,
   The sheep and cattle on the leas;
   The houses up the hills, the trees—

84. Thou comest, May

THOU comest, May, with leaves and flowers,
   And nights grow short, and days grow long;
And for thy sake in bush and tree,
   The small birds sing, both old and young;
And only I am dumb and wait
The passing of a fish-like state.

You birds, you old grandfathers now,
   That have such power to welcome spring,
I, but a father in my years,
   Have nothing in my mind to sing;
My lips, like gills in deep-sea homes,
Beat time, and still no music comes.

85. The Best Friend

NOW shall I walk
　Or shall I ride?
" Ride," Pleasure said;
　" Walk," Joy replied.

Now what shall I—
　Stay home or roam?
" Roam," Pleasure said;
　And Joy—" Stay home."

Now shall I dance,
　Or sit for dreams?
" Sit," answers Joy;
　" Dance," Pleasure screams.

Which of ye two
　Will kindest be?
Pleasure laughed sweet,
　But Joy kissed me.

86. Rich Days

WELCOME to you rich Autumn days,
    Ere comes the cold, leaf-picking wind;
When golden stooks are seen in fields,
    All standing arm-in-arm entwined;
And gallons of sweet cider seen
On trees in apples red and green.

With mellow pears that cheat our teeth,
    Which melt that tongues may suck them in;
With blue-black damsons, yellow plums,
    Now sweet and soft from stone to skin;
And woodnuts rich, to make us go
Into the loneliest lanes we know.

HERE comes Kate Summers who, for gold,
    Takes any man to bed:
" You know my friend, Nell Barnes," said she;
    " You knew Nell Barnes—she's dead.

" Nell Barnes was bad on all you men,
    Unclean, a thief as well;
Yet all my life I have not found
    A better friend than Nell.

" So I sat at her side at last,
    For hours, till she was dead;
And yet she had no sense at all
    Of any word I said.

" For all her cry but came to this—
    'Not for the world!   Take care:
Don't touch that bird of paradise,
    Perched on the bed-post there!'

" I asked her would she like some grapes,
    Some damsons ripe and sweet;
A custard made with new-laid eggs,

"I promised I would follow her,
  To see her in her grave;
And buy a wreath with borrowed pence,
  If nothing I could save.

" Yet still her cry but came to this—
  'Not for the world! Take care:
Don't touch that bird of paradise,
  Perched on the bed-post there!'"

88.   This World

WHO dreams a sweeter life than this,
    To stand and stare, when at this fence,
Back into those dumb creatures' eyes,
    And think we have their innocence—
Our looks as open as the skies.

Lambs with their legs and noses black,
    Whose woolly necks, so soft and white,
Can take away the children's breath;
    Who'd strangle them in their delight—
And calves they'd worry half to death.

This world's too full of those dull men
    Who ne'er advance from that first state
Which opens mouths before the eye;
    Who, when they think of dumb things, rate
Them by the body's gluttony.

89. The Lodging House Fire

MY birthday—yesterday,
     Its hours were twenty-four;
Four hours I lived lukewarm,
And killed a score.

Eight bells and then I woke,
Came to our fire below,
Then sat four hours and watched
Its sullen glow.

Then out four hours I walked,
The lukewarm four I live,
And felt no other joy
Than air can give.

My mind durst know no thought,
It knew my life too well:
'Twas hell before, behind,
And round me hell.

Back to that fire again,
Six hours I watch it now,
And take to bed dim eyes
And fever's brow

The Lodging House Fire

Ten hours I give to sleep,
More than my need, I know;
But I escape my mind
And that fire's glow.

For listen : it is death
To watch that fire's glow;
For, as it burns more red
Men paler grow.

O better in foul room
That's warm, make life away,
Than homeless out of doors,
Cold night and day.

Pile on the coke, make fire,
Rouse its death-dealing glow;
Men are borne dead away
Ere they can know.

I lie; I cannot watch
Its glare from hour to hour;
It makes one sleep, to wake
Out of my power.

I close my eyes and swear
It shall not wield its power;
No use, I wake to find
A murdered hour

Lying between us there!
That fire drowsed me deep,
And I wrought murder's deed—
Did it in sleep.

I count us, thirty men,
Huddled from Winter's blow,
Helpless to move away
From that fire's glow.

So goes my life each day—
Its hours are twenty-four—
Four hours I live lukewarm,
And kill a score.

No man lives life so wise
But unto Time he throws
Morsels to hunger for
At his life's close.

Were all such morsels heaped—
Time greedily devours,
When man sits still—he'd mourn
So few wise hours.

But all my day is waste,
I live a lukewarm four
And make a red coke fire
Poison the score.

90. Body and Spirit

WHO stands before me on the stairs:
   Ah, is it you, my love?
My candle-light burns through your arm,
   And still thou dost not move;
Thy body's dead, this is not you—
It is thy ghost my light burns through.

Thy spirit this: I leap the stairs,
   To reach thy body's place;
I kiss and kiss, and still there comes
   No colour to thy face;
I hug thee for one little breath—
For this is sleep, it is not death!

   *   *   *   *

The first night she was in her grave,
   And I looked in the glass,
I saw her sit upright in bed—
   Without a sound it was;
I saw her hand feel in the cloth,
To fetch a box of powder forth.

Body and Spirit

She sat and watched me all the while,
  For fear I looked her way;
I saw her powder cheek and chin,
  Her fast corrupting clay;
Then down my lady lay, and smiled—
She thought her beauty saved, poor child.

Now down the stairs I leap half-mad,
  And up the street I start;
I still can see her hand at work,
  And oh, it breaks my heart:
All night behind my back I see
Her powdering, with her eyes on me.

91.   Love's Coming

AN hour or more she's gone,
And we are left alone,
I and her bird.
At last he twittered sweet,
To hear my loved one's feet,
And I, too, heard.

When she had entered there
He cocked his head with care,
If right or wrong;
But when her voice was heard
A frenzy seized the bird
To rave in song.

"Peace, pet, my love is near,
Her voice I cannot hear
In such a din;
Thou couldst not call more loud
Unto a smiling cloud
That May hides in."

Now, what his thoughts could be
If she still spake and he
In harmony;
Or had forgetful grown,
Enamoured of his own
Sweet melody—

I do not know; I know
I out with her must go
To hear her story.
We left that raving thing—
Made worse by laughter—sing
Out his mad glory.

THE little ones are put in bed,
  And both are laughing, lying down;
Their father, and their mother too,
  Are gone on Christmas-eve to town.

"Old Santa Claus will bring a horse,
  Gee up!" cried little Will, with glee;
"If I am good, I'll have a doll
  From Santa Claus"—laughed Emily.

The little ones are gone to sleep,
  Their father and their mother now
Are coming home, with many more—
  They're drunk, and make a merry row.

The little ones on Christmas morn
  Jump up, like skylarks from the grass;
And then they stand as still as stones,
  And just as cold as stones, alas!

No horse, no doll beside their bed,
  No sadder little ones could be;
"We did some wrong," said little Will—

93.   Where we Differ

TO think my thoughts all hers,
    Not one of hers is mine;
She laughs—while I must sigh;
    She sings—while I must whine.

She eats—while I must fast;
    She reads—while I am blind;
She sleeps—while I must wake;
    Free—I no freedom find.

To think the world for me
    Contains but her alone,
And that her eyes prefer
    Some ribbon, scarf, or stone.

94.   Parted

ALACK for life !
 Worn to a stalk since yesterday
Is the flower with whom the bee did stay,
And he was but one night away.
Alack for life, I say.

Alack for life!
A flower put on her fine array,
In hopes a bee would come her way,
Who's dying in his hive this day.
Alack for life, I say.

Alack for life !
If Death like Love would throw his dart
And pierce at once a double heart,
And not to strike away one part—
Alack for life, who'd say?

95.　The Blind Boxer

HE goes with basket, and slow feet,
　　To sell his nuts from street to street;
The very terror of his kind,
Till blackened eyes had made him blind.
Aye, this is Boxer Bob, the man
That had hard muscles harder than
A schoolboy's bones; who held his ground
When six tall bullies sparred around.
Small children now, that have no grace,
Can steal his nuts before his face;
And, when he threatens with his hands,
Mock him two feet from where he stands;
Mock him who could, some years ago,
Have leapt five feet to strike a blow.
Poor Bobby, I remember when
Thou wert a god to drunken men;
But now they push thee off, or crack
Thy nuts and give no money back;
They swear they'll strike thee in the face,
Dost thou not hurry from that place;
Such are the men that once would pay

The Blind Boxer

With all thy strength and cunning skill,
Thy courage, lasting breath, and will,
Thou'rt helpless now; a little ball,
No bigger than a cherry small,
Has now refused to guide and lead
Twelve stone of strong, hard flesh that need
But that ball's light to make thee leap
And strike these cowards down like sheep.
Poor, helpless Bobby, blind: I see
Thy working face and pity thee.

96.   Now

WHEN I was in yon town, and had
    Stones all round me, hard and cold,
My flesh was firm, my sight was keen,
    And still I felt my heart grow old.

But now, with this green world around,
    By my great love for it! I swear,
Though my flesh shrink, and my sight fail,
    My heart will not grow old with care.

When I do hear these joyful birds,
    I cannot sit with my heart dumb;
I cannot walk among these flowers,
    But I must help the bees to hum.

My heart has echoes for all things,
    The wind, the rain, the bird and bee;
'Tis I that—now—can carry Time,
    Who in that town must carry me.

I see not now the great coke fire
    With ten men seated there, or more,
Like frogs on logs; and one man fall
    Dying across the boarded floor.

Now

I see instead the flowers and clouds,
   I hear the rills, the birds and bees :
The Squirrel flies before the storm
   He makes himself in leafy trees.

MY Fancy loves to play with Clouds
That hour by hour can change Heaven's face;
For I am sure of my delight,
    In green or stony place.

Sometimes they on tall mountains pile
    Mountains of silver, twice as high;
And then they break and lie like rocks
    All over the wide sky.

And then I see flocks very fair;
    And sometimes, near their fleeces white,
Are small black lambs that soon will grow
    And hide their mothers quite.

Sometimes, like little fishes, they
    Are all one size, and one great shoal;
Sometimes they like big sailing ships
    Across the blue sky roll.

Sometimes I see small Cloudlets tow
    Big, heavy Clouds across those skies—
Like little Ants that carry off

Clouds

Sometimes I see at morn bright Clouds
  That stand so still, they make me stare;
It seems as they had trained all night
  To make no motion there.

98.   The Posts

A YEAR'S a post, on which
    It saith
The distance—growing less—
    To Death.

Some posts I missed, beguiled
    By Song
And Beauty, as I passed
    Along.

But sad am I to think
    This day
Of forty posts passed on
    My way.

For not one post I now
    Must pass
Will 'scape these eyes of mine,
    Alas !

99.   No Master

INDEED this is sweet life! my hand
   Is under no proud man's command;
There is no voice to break my rest
Before a bird has left its nest;
There is no man to change my mood,
Would I go nutting in the wood;
No man to pluck my sleeve and say—
I want thy labour for this day;
No man to keep me out of sight,
When that dear Sun is shining bright.
None but my friends shall have command
Upon my time, my heart and hand;
I'll rise from sleep to help a friend,
But let no stranger orders send,
Or hear my curses fast and thick,
Which in his purse-proud throat will stick
Like burs.   If I cannot be free
To do such work as pleases me,
Near woodland pools and under trees,
You'll get no work at all; for I
Would rather live this life and die
A beggar or a thief, than be

100. Rich or Poor

WITH thy true love I have more wealth
   Than Charon's piled-up bank doth hold;
Where he makes kings lay down their crowns
   And lifelong misers leave their gold.

Without thy love I've no more wealth
   Than seen upon that other shore;
That cold, bare bank he rows them to—
   Those kings and misers made so poor.

101. The Sea

HER cheeks were white, her eyes were wild,
Her heart was with her sea-gone child.
"Men say you know and love the sea?
It is ten days, my child left me;
Ten days, and still he doth not come,
And I am weary of my home."

I thought of waves that ran the deep
And flashed like rabbits, when they leap,
The white part of their tails; the glee
Of captains that take brides to sea,
And own the ships they steer; how seas
Played leap-frog over ships with ease.

The great Sea-Wind, so rough and kind;
Ho, ho! his strength; the great Sea-Wind
Blows iron tons across the sea!
Ho, ho! his strength; how wild and free!
He breaks the waves, to our amaze,
Into ten thousand little sprays!

"Nay, have no fear"; I laughed with joy,

The Sea's wild horses, they are far
More safe than Land's tamed horses are;
They kick with padded hoofs, and bite
With teeth that leave no marks in sight.

" True, Waves will howl when, all day long
The Wind keeps piping loud and strong ;
For in ship's sails the wild Sea-Breeze
Pipes sweeter than your birds in trees;
But have no fear "—I laughed with joy,
" That you have lost a sea-gone boy."

That night I saw ten thousand bones
Coffined in ships, in weeds and stones;
Saw how the Sea's strong jaws could take
Big iron ships like rats to shake;
Heard him still moan his discontent
For one man or a continent.

I saw that woman go from place
To place, hungry for her child's face;
I heard her crying, crying, crying;
Then, in a flash! saw the Sea trying,
With savage joy, and efforts wild,
To smash his rocks with a dead child.

102.   A Life's Love

HOW do I love to sit and dream
　　Of that sweet passion, when I meet
The lady I must love for life!
　The very thought makes my Soul beat
Its wings, as though it saw that light
Silver the rims of my black night.

I see her bring a crimson mouth
　　To open at a kiss, and close;
I see her bring her two fair cheeks,
　　That I may paint on each a rose;
I see her two hands, like doves white,
Fly into mine and hide from sight.

In fancy hear her soft, sweet voice;
　　My eager Soul, to catch her words,
Waits at the ear, with Noah's haste
　　To take God's message-bearing birds;
What passion she will in me move—
The Lady I for life must love!

103.   April's Boys and Girls

OF primrose boys
    April has many;
He seems as fond
    Of them as any;
He shows the world
Those boys in gold.

But violets are
    His girls, whom he
Shuts up in some
    Green nunnery:
So does he prove
His deepest love.

April, a girl
    Of yours is found;
High walls of grass
    Hemmed her around:
April, forgive me—
I followed a bee.

104.   Sweet Child

SWEET child, that wast my bird by day,
   My bird that never failed in song;
That on my bosom wast a bee,
   And layst there all night long:

No more I'll hear thy voice at noon,
   For Death has pierced thee with a thorn
No more thou'lt sleep upon my breast,
   And trample it at morn.

Then break, oh break, poor empty cage,
   The bird is dead, thy use is done;
And die, poor plant, for your sweet bee
   Is gone, forever gone.

105.   Death's Game

DEATH can but play one game with me—
   If I live here alone;
He cannot strike me a foul blow
   Through a belovèd one.

To-day he takes my neighbour's wife,
   And leaves a little child
To lie upon his breast and cry
   Like the Night-wind, so wild.

And every hour its voice is heard—
   Tell me where is she gone!
Death cannot play that game with me—
   If I live here alone.

106.   Sweet Youth

AND art thou gone, sweet Youth? Say Nay!
For thou dost know what power was thine,
That thou couldst give vain shadows flesh,
And laughter without any wine,
From the heart fresh?

And art thou gone, sweet Youth? Say Nay!
Not left me to Time's cruel spite;
He'll pull my teeth out one by one,
He'll paint my hair first grey, then white,
He'll scrape my bone.

And art thou gone, sweet Youth? Alas!
For ever gone! I know it well;
Earth has no atom, nor the sky,
That has not thrown the kiss Farewell—
Sweet Youth, Good-Bye!

107.   A Plain Life

NO idle gold—since this fine sun, my friend,
 Is no mean miser, but doth freely spend.

No precious stones—since these green mornings show,
Without a change, their pearls where'er I go.

No lifeless books—since birds with their sweet tongues
Will read aloud to me their happier songs.

No painted scenes—since clouds can change their skies
A hundred times a day to please my eyes.

No headstrong wine—since, while I drink, the spring
Into my eager ears will softly sing.

No surplus clothes—since every simple beast
Can teach me to be happy with the least.

108.　　Heaven

THAT paradise the Arab dreams,
　　Is for less sand and more fresh streams.
The only heaven an Indian knows,
Is hunting deer and buffaloes.
The Yankee heaven—to bring Fame forth
By some freak show of what he's worth.
The heaven that fills an English heart,
Is Union Jacks in every part.
The Irish heaven is heaven of old,
When Satan cracked skulls manifold.
The Scotsman has his heaven to come—
To argue his Creator dumb.
The Welshman's heaven is singing airs—
No matter who feels sick and swears.

109.   Ale

NOW do I hear thee weep and groan,
   Who hath a comrade sunk at sea?
Then quaff thee of my good old ale,
   And it will raise him up for thee;
Thou'lt think as little of him then
As when he moved with living men.

If thou hast hopes to move the world,
   And every effort it doth fail,
Then to thy side call Jack and Jim,
   And bid them drink with thee good ale;
So may the world, that would not hear,
Perish in hell with all your care.

One quart of good old ale, and I
   Feel then what life immortal is:
The brain is empty of all thought,
   The heart is brimming o'er with bliss;
Time's first child, Life, doth live; but Death,
The second, hath not yet his breath.

Ale

Give me a quart of good old ale,
    Am I a homeless man on earth?
Nay, I want not your roof and quilt,
    I'll lie warm at the moon's cold hearth;
No grumbling ghost to grudge my bed,
His grave, ha! ha! holds up my head.

110.   A Fleeting Passion

THOU shalt not laugh, thou shalt not romp,
    Let's grimly kiss with bated breath;
As quietly and solemnly
    As Life when it is kissing Death.
Now in the silence of the grave,
    My hand is squeezing that soft breast;
While thou dost in such passion lie,
    It mocks me with its look of rest.

But when the morning comes at last,
    And we must part, our passions cold,
You'll think of some new feather, scarf
    To buy with my small piece of gold;
And I'll be dreaming of green lanes,
    Where little things with beating hearts
Hold shining eyes between the leaves,
    'Till men with horses pass, and carts.

111. The Child and the Mariner

A DEAR old couple my grandparents were,
    And kind to all dumb things; they saw in Heave
The lamb that Jesus petted when a child;
Their faith was never draped by Doubt: to them
Death was a rainbow in Eternity,
That promised everlasting brightness soon.
An old seafaring man was he; a rough
Old man, but kind; and hairy, like the nut
Full of sweet milk.   All day on shore he watched
The winds for sailors' wives, and told what ships
Enjoyed fair weather, and what ships had storms;
He watched the sky, and he could tell for sure
What afternoons would follow stormy morns,
If quiet nights would end wild afternoons.
He leapt away from scandal with a roar,
And if a whisper still possessed his mind,
He walked about and cursed it for a plague.
He took offence at Heaven when beggars passed,
And sternly called them back to give them help.

In this old captain's house I lived, and things
That house contained were in ships' cabins once:

Green weeds, dried fishes stuffed, and coral stalks;
Old wooden trunks with handles of spliced rope,
With copper saucers full of monies strange,
That seemed the savings of dead men, not touched
To keep them warm since their real owners died;
Strings of red beads, methought were dipped in blood,
And swinging lamps, as though the house might move;
An ivory lighthouse built on ivory rocks,
The bones of fishes and three bottled ships.
And many a thing was there which sailors make
In idle hours, when on long voyages,
Of marvellous patience, to no lovely end.
And on those charts I saw the small black dots
That were called islands, and I knew they had
Turtles and palms, and pirates' buried gold.

There came a stranger to my grandad's house,
The old man's nephew, a seafarer too;
A big, strong able man who could have walked
Twm Barlum's hill all clad in iron mail;
So strong he could have made one man his club
To knock down others—Henry was his name,
No other name was uttered by his kin.
And here he was, insooth ill-clad, but oh,
Thought I, what secrets of the sea are his!
This man knows coral islands in the sea,
And dusky girls heartbroken for white men;

156 The Child and the Mariner

This sailor knows of wondrous lands afar,
More rich than Spain, when the Phœnicians shipped
Silver for common ballast, and they saw
Horses at silver mangers eating grain;
This man has seen the wind blow up a mermaid's hair
Which, like a golden serpent, reared and stretched
To feel the air away beyond her head.
He begged my pennies, which I gave with joy—
He will most certainly return sometime
A self-made king of some new land, and rich.
Alas that he, the hero of my dreams,
Should be his people's scorn; for they had grown
To proud command of ships, whilst he had toiled
Before the mast for years, and well content;
Him they despised, and only Death could bring
A likeness in his face to show like them.
For he drank all his pay, nor went to sea
As long as ale was easy got on shore.

Now, in his last long voyage he had sailed
From Plymouth Sound to where sweet odours fan
The Cingalese at work, and then back home—
But came not near his kin till pay was spent.
He was not old, yet seemed so; for his face
Looked like the drowned man's in the morgue, when it
Has struck the wooden wharves and keels of ships.
And all his flesh was pricked with Indian ink.

His body marked as rare and delicate
As dead men struck by lightning under trees,
And pictured with fine twigs and curlèd ferns;
Chains on his neck and anchors on his arms;
Rings on his fingers, bracelets on his wrist;
And on his breast the Jane of Appledore
Was schooner rigged, and in full sail at sea.
He could not whisper with his strong hoarse voice,
No more than could a horse creep quietly;
He laughed to scorn the men that muffled close
For fear of wind, till all their neck was hid,
Like Indian corn wrapped up in long green leaves.
He knew no flowers but seaweeds brown and green,
He knew no birds but those that followed ships.
Full well he knew the water-world; he heard
A grander music there than we on land,
When organ shakes a church; swore he would make
The sea his home, though it was always roused
By such wild storms as never leave Cape Horn;
Happy to hear the tempest grunt and squeal
Like pigs heard dying in a slaughterhouse.
A true-born mariner, and this his hope—
His coffin would be what his cradle was,
A boat to drown in and be sunk at sea;
To drown at sea and lie a dainty corpse
Salted and iced in Neptune's larder deep.
This man despised small coasters, fishing smacks;

He scorned those sailors who at night and morn
Can see the coast, when in their little boats
They go a six days' voyage and are back
Home with their wives for every Sabbath day.
Much did he talk of tankards of old beer,
And bottled stuff he drank in other lands,
Which was a liquid fire like Hell to gulp,
But Paradise to sip.

                      And so he talked;
Nor did those people listen with more awe
To Lazarus—whom they had seen stone dead—
Than did we urchins to that seaman's voice.
He many a tale of wonder told : of where,
At Argostoli, Cephalonia's sea
Ran over the earth's lip in heavy floods;
And then again of how the strange Chinese
Conversed much as our homely Blackbirds sing.
He told us how he sailed in one old ship
Near that volcano Martinique, whose power
Shook like dry leaves the whole Caribbean seas,
And made the Sun set in a sea of fire
Which only half was his ; and dust was thick
On deck, and stones were pelted at the mast.
So, as we walked along, that seaman dropped
Into my greedy ears such words that sleep
Stood at my pillow half the night perplexed.

He told how isles sprang up and sank again,
Between short voyages, to his amaze;
How they did come and go, and cheated charts;
Told how a crew was cursed when one man killed
A bird that perched upon a moving barque;
And how the sea's sharp needles, firm and strong,
Ripped open the bellies of big, iron ships;
Of mighty icebergs in the Northern seas,
That haunt the far horizon like white ghosts.
He told of waves that lift a ship so high
That birds could pass from starboard unto port
Under her dripping keel.

           Oh, it was sweet
To hear that seaman tell such wondrous tales:
How deep the sea in parts, that drownèd men
Must go a long way to their graves and sink
Day after day, and wander with the tides.
He spake of his own deeds; of how he sailed
One summer's night along the Bosphorus,
And he,—who knew no music like the wash
Of waves against a ship, or wind in shrouds—
Heard then the music on that woody shore
Of nightingales, and feared to leave the deck,
He thought 'twas sailing into Paradise.

To hear these stories all we urchins placed

Our pennies in that seaman's ready hand;
Until one morn he signed for a long cruise,
And sailed away—we never saw him more.
Could such a man sink in the sea unknown?
Nay, he had found a land with something rich,
That kept his eyes turned inland for his life
" A damn bad sailor and a landshark too,
No good in port or out '—my grandad said.

PRINTED BY WILLIAM PRENDON AND SON, LTD
PLYMOUTH, ENGLAND

Printed in the USA
CPSIA information can be obtained
at www.ICGtesting.com
LVHW010745220124
769586LV00036B/913